Faces and Accessories

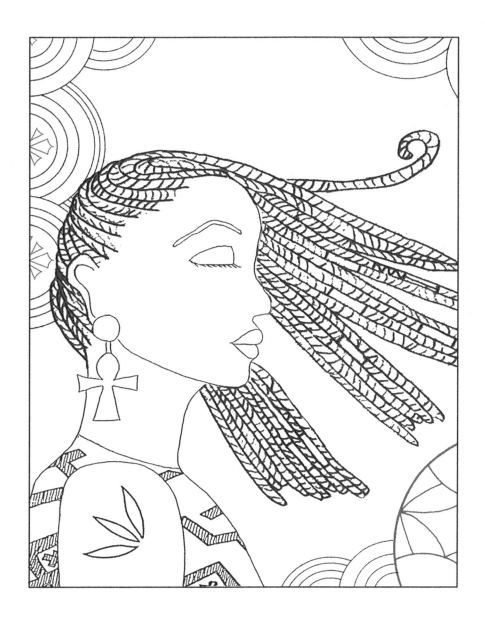

by Anne Bruno

Thank you for your purchase. I hope you will have fun coloring the following designs. I've certainly enjoyed creating them.

I would love to hear from you. Your feedback is important. Feel free to conact me at:

http://annebrunoart.com

Facebook and Instagram: @annebrunoart

Anne

Color test sheet

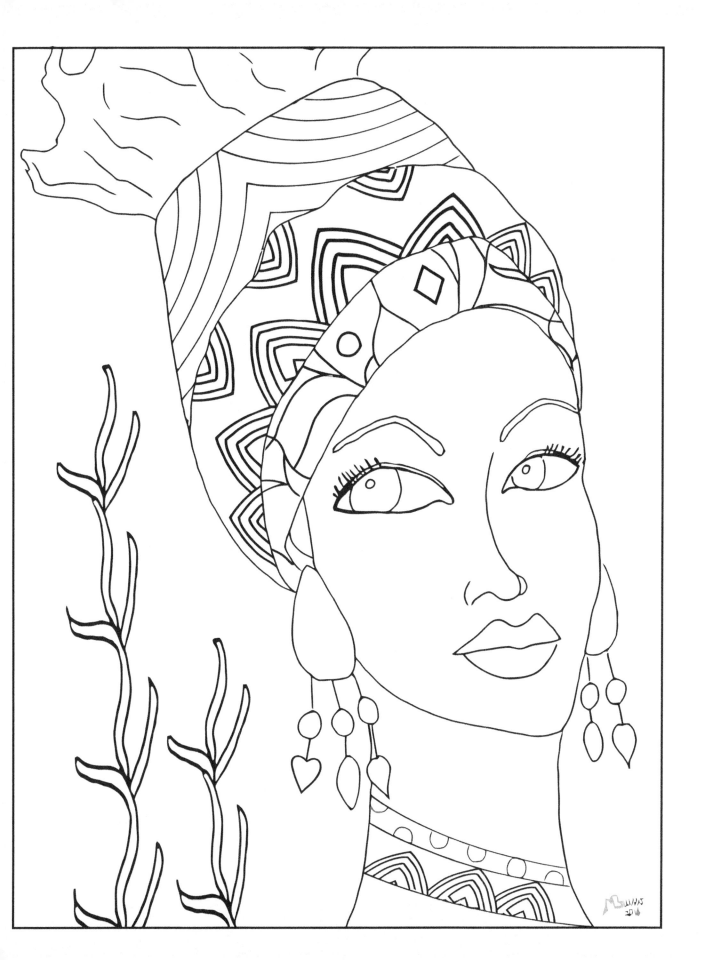

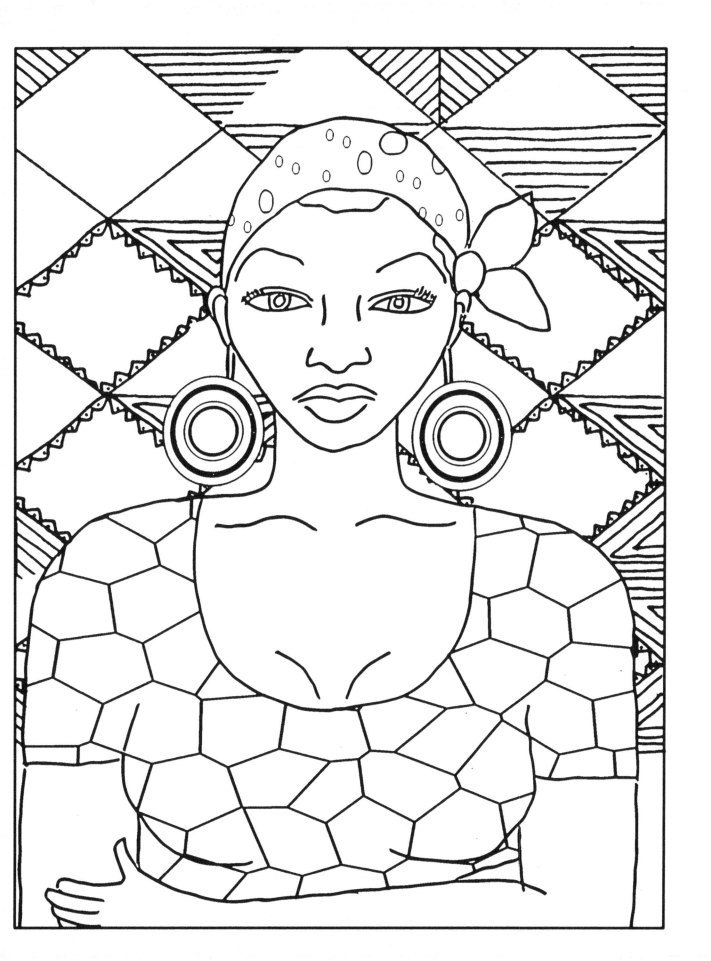

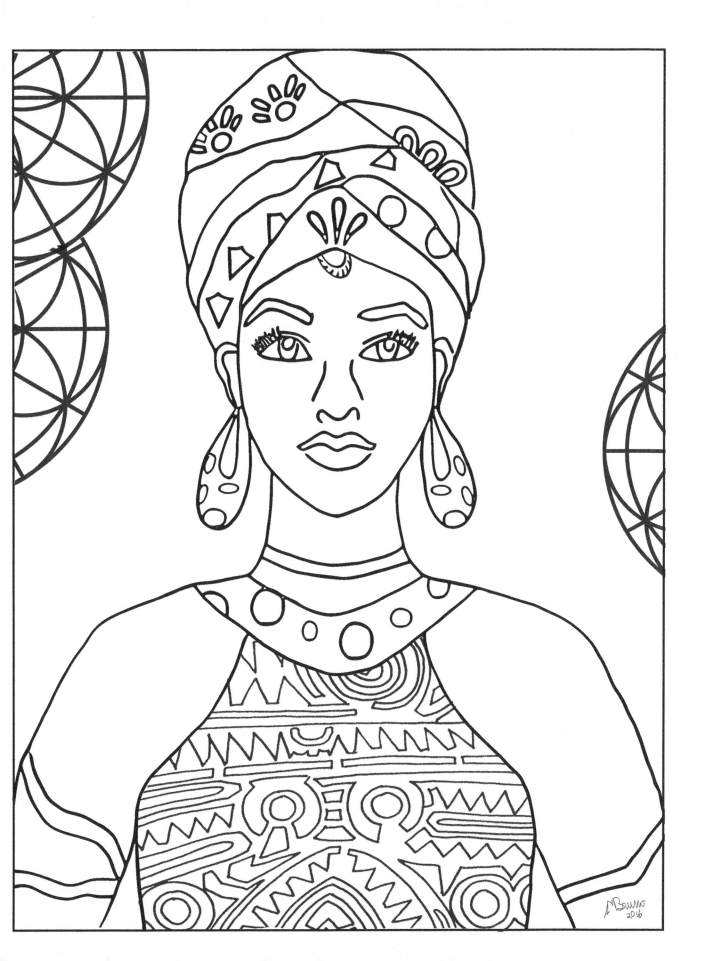

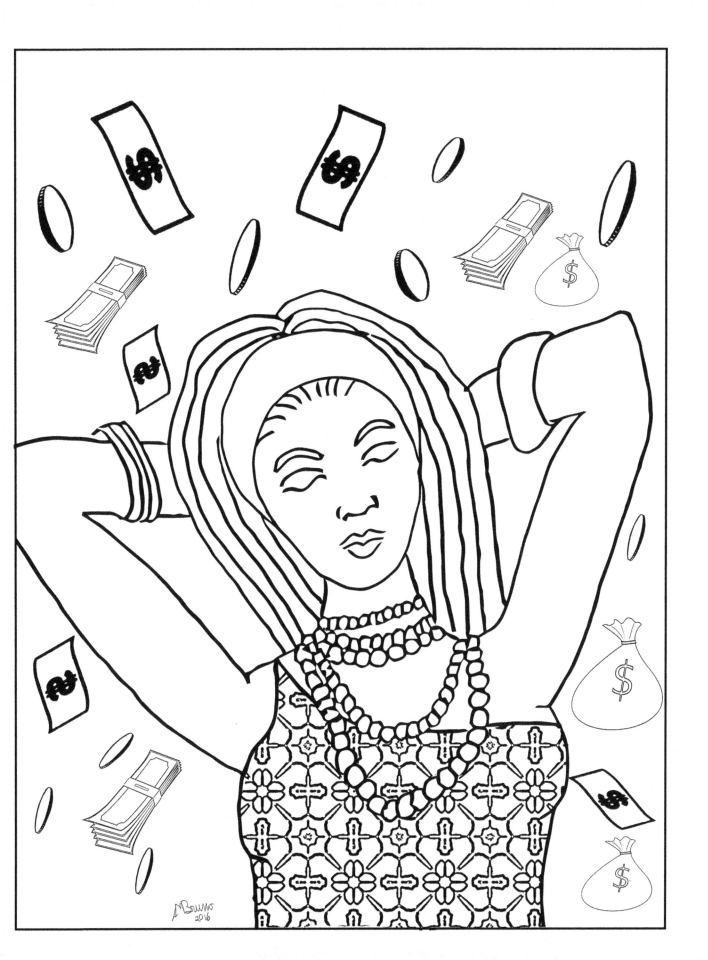

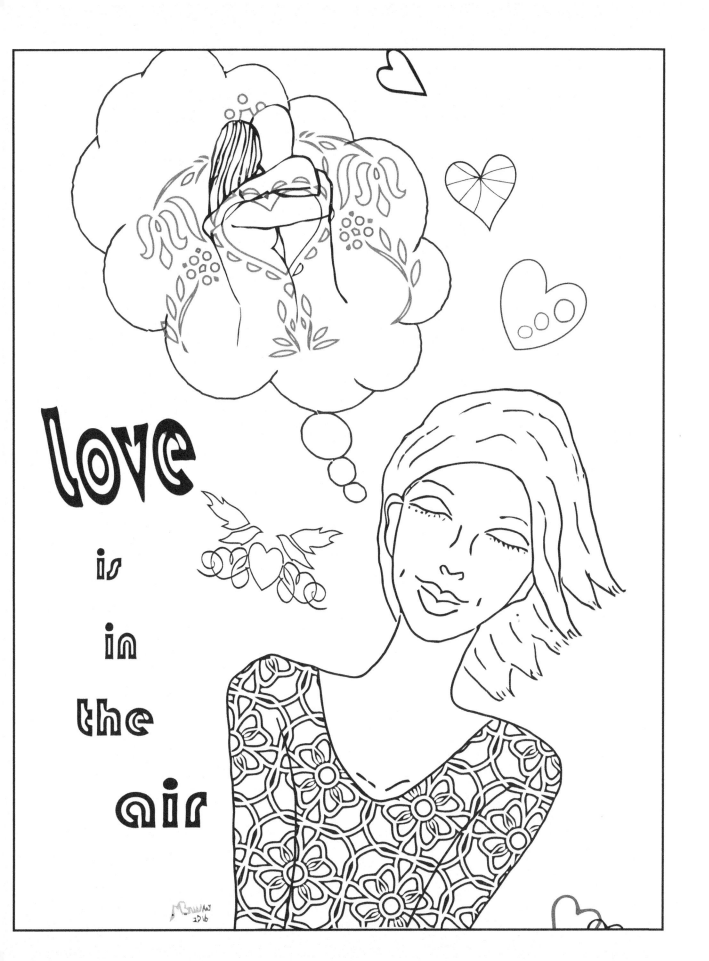

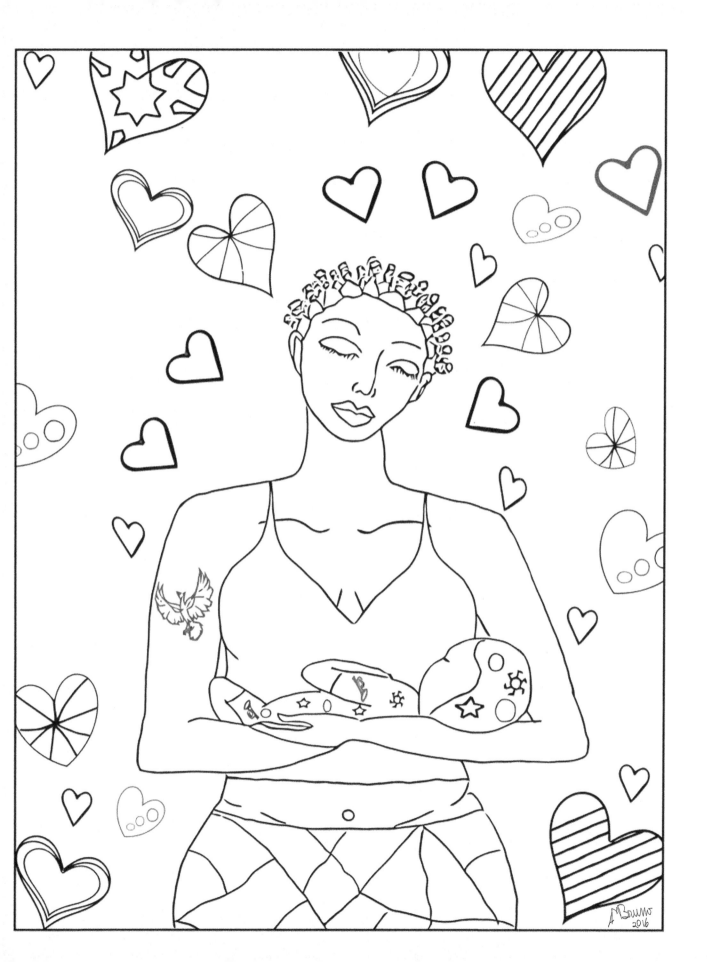

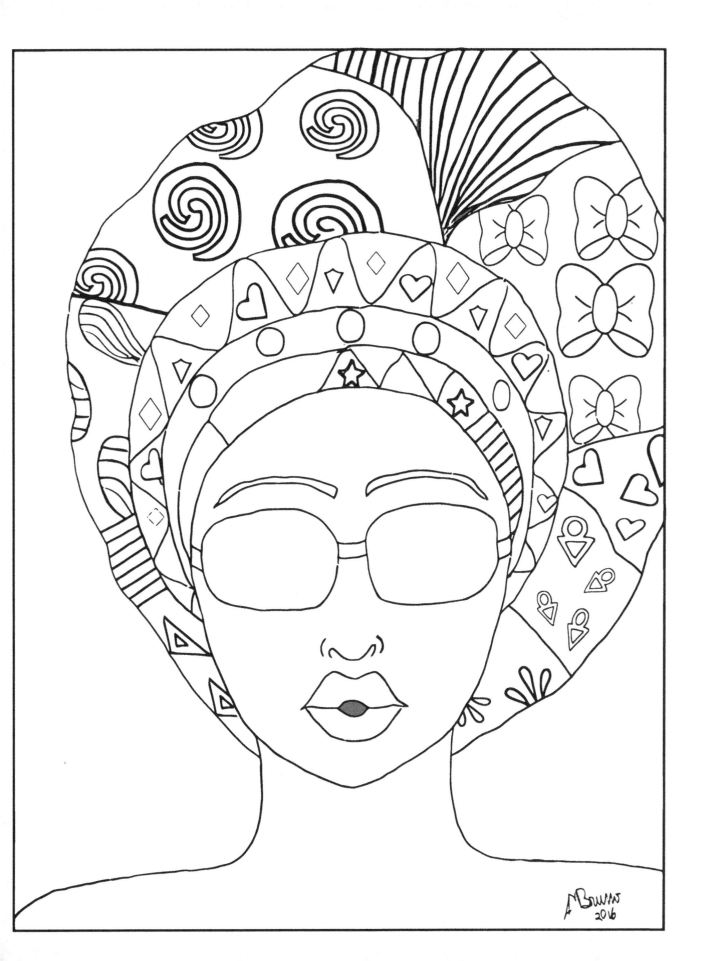

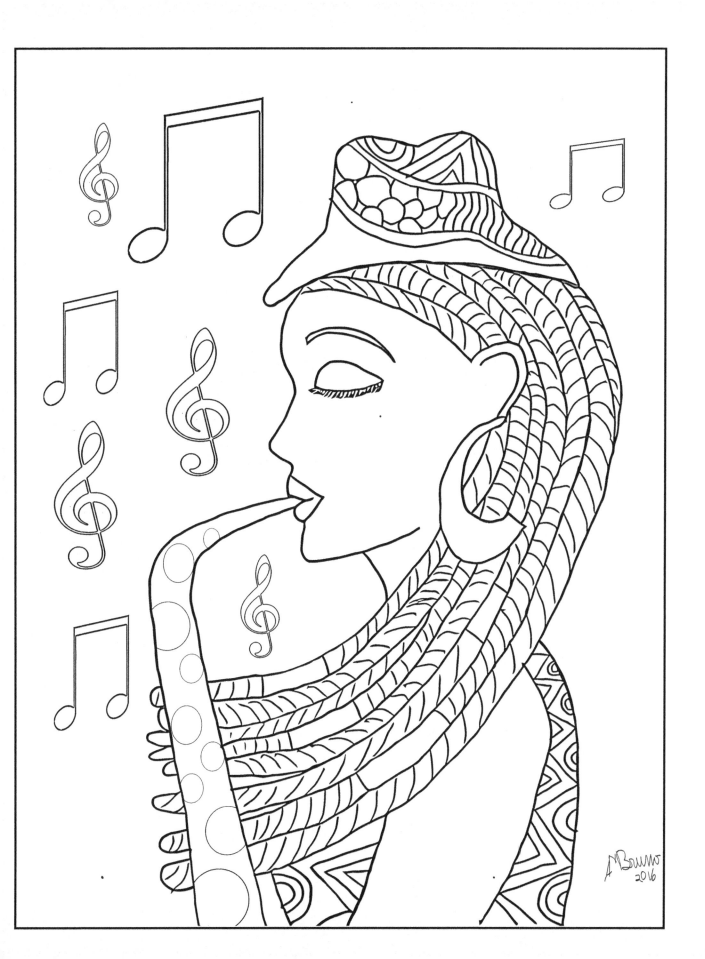

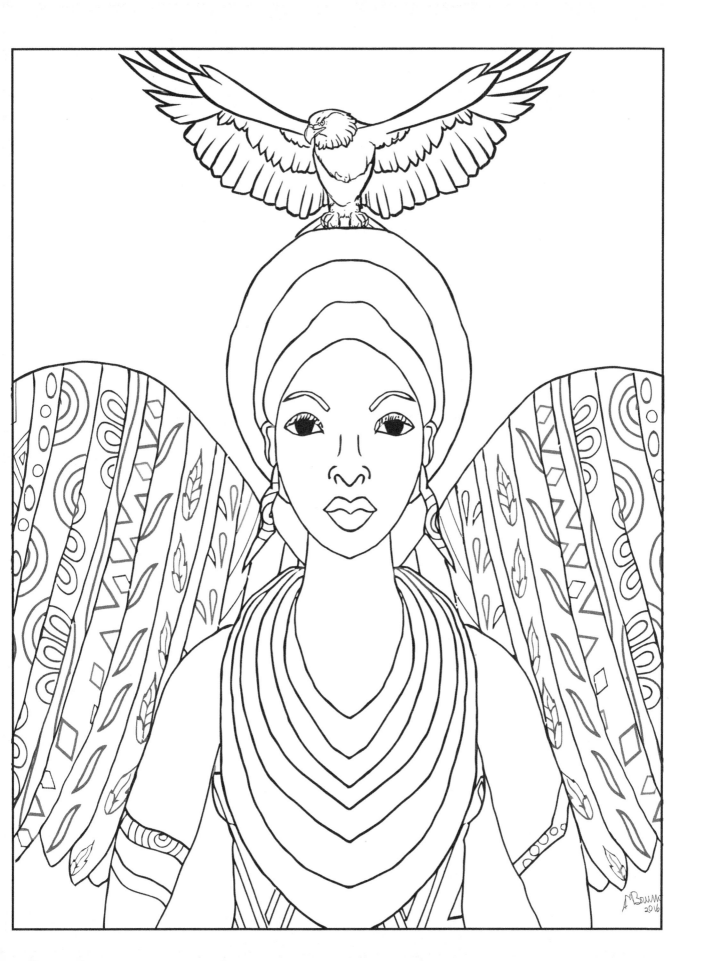

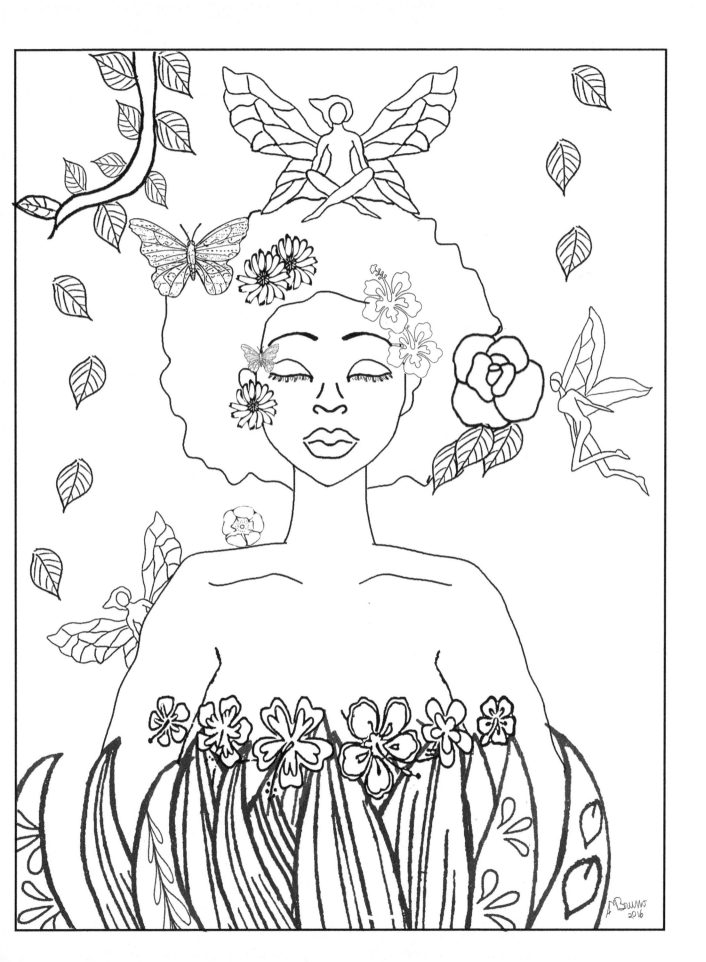

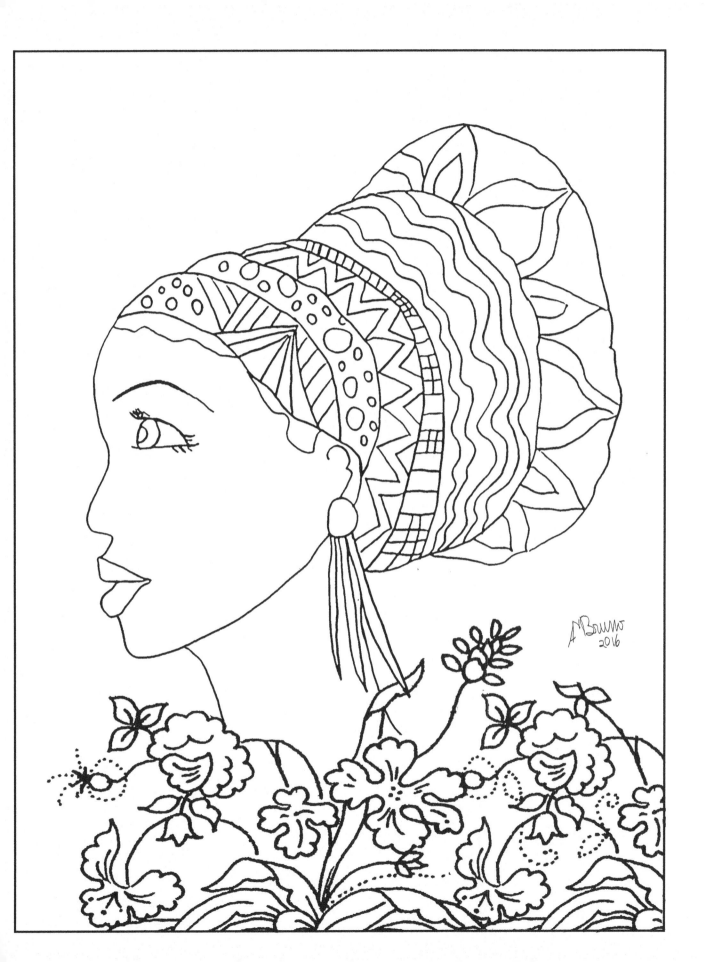

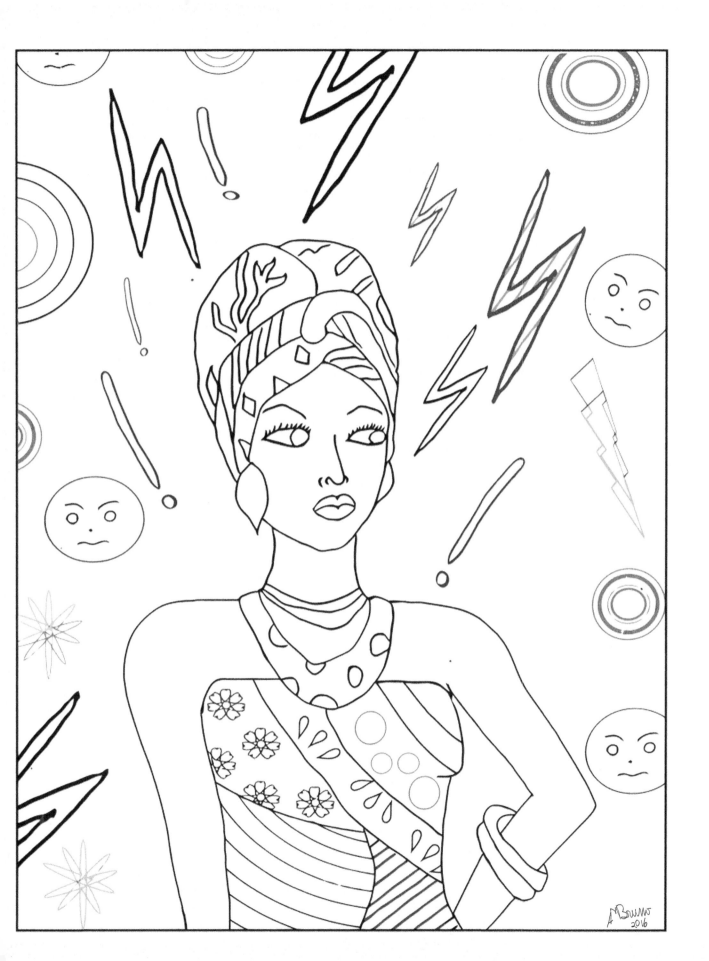

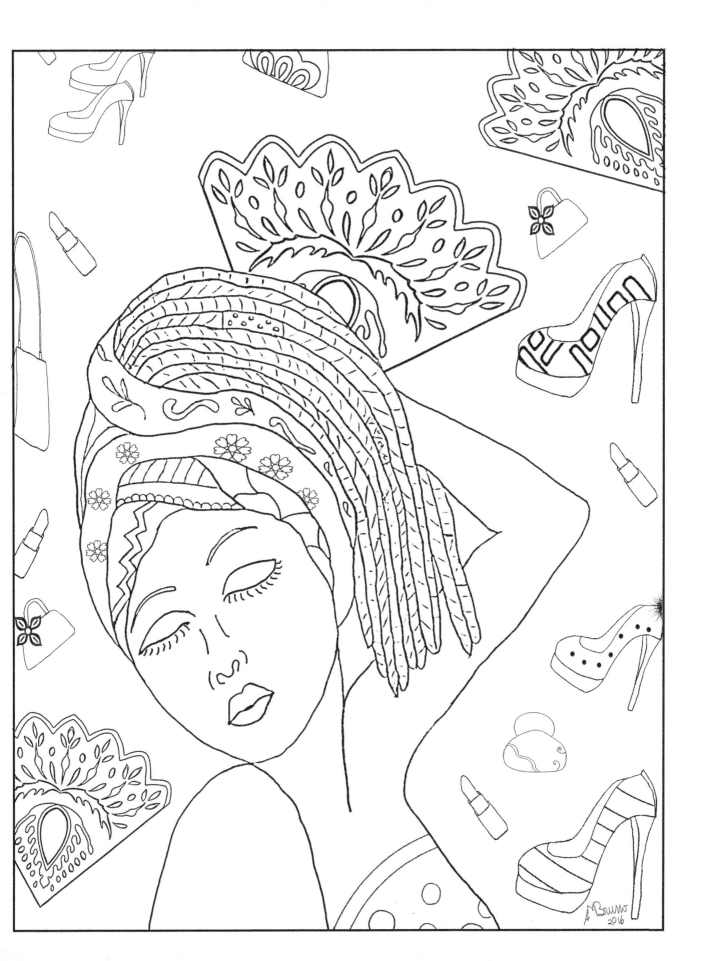

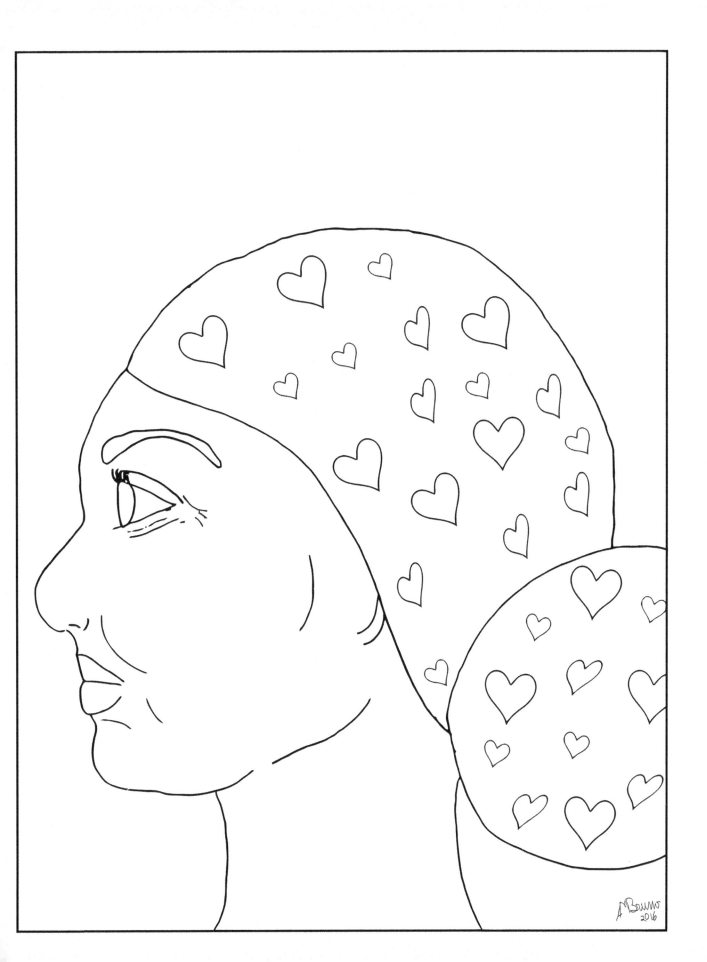

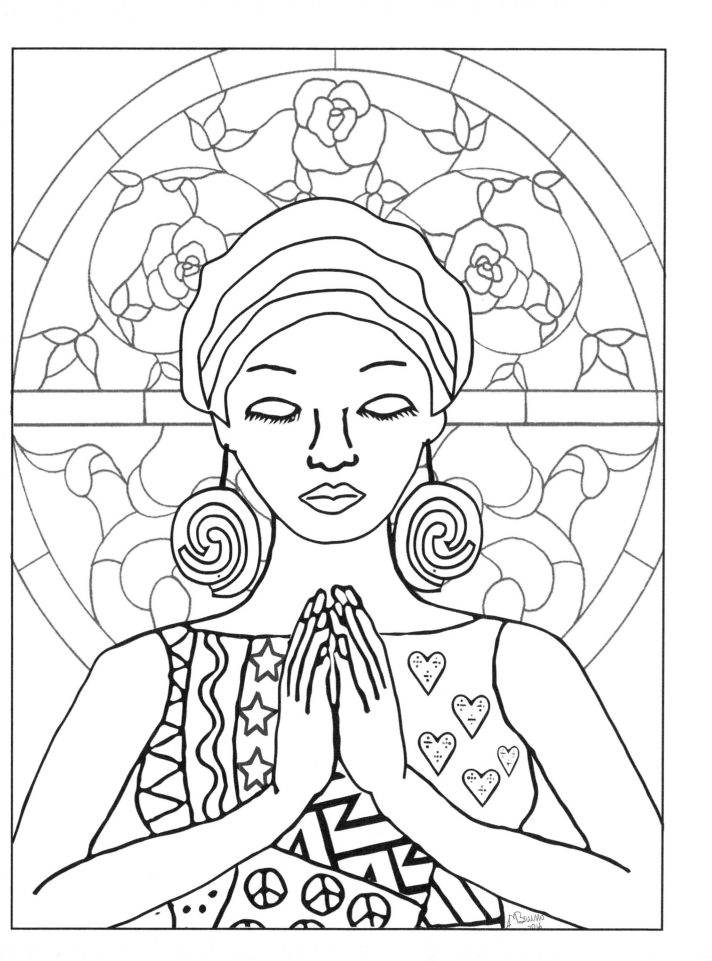

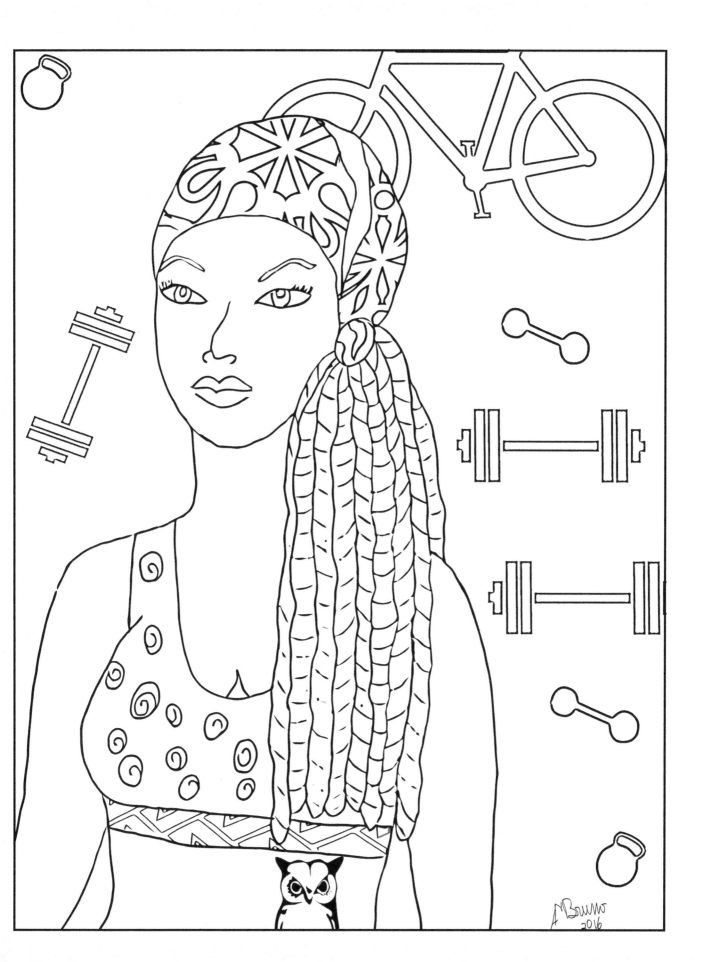

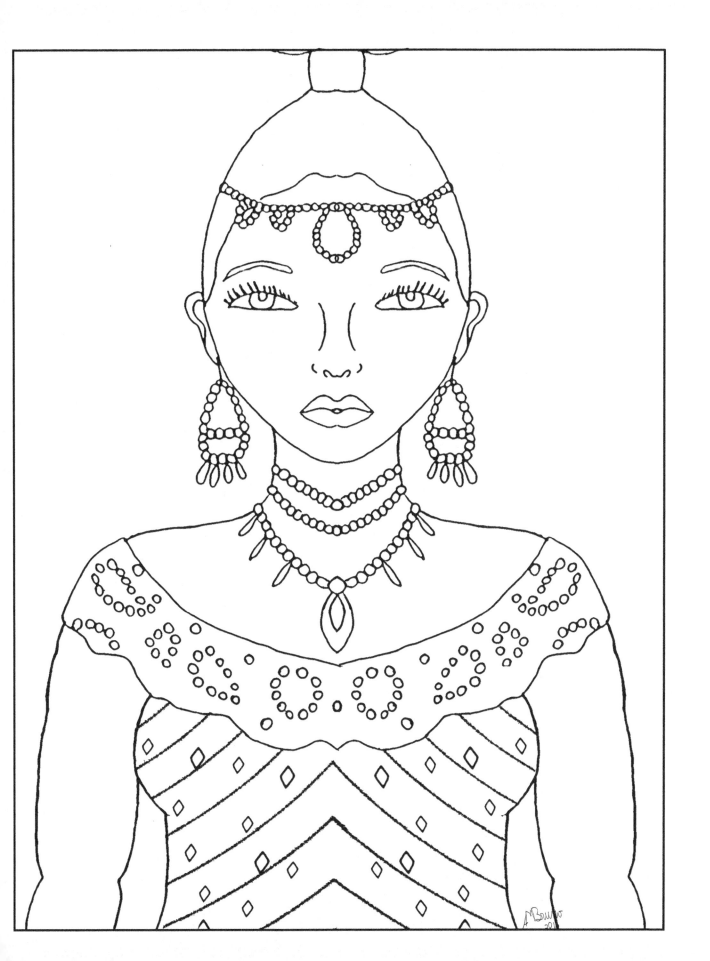

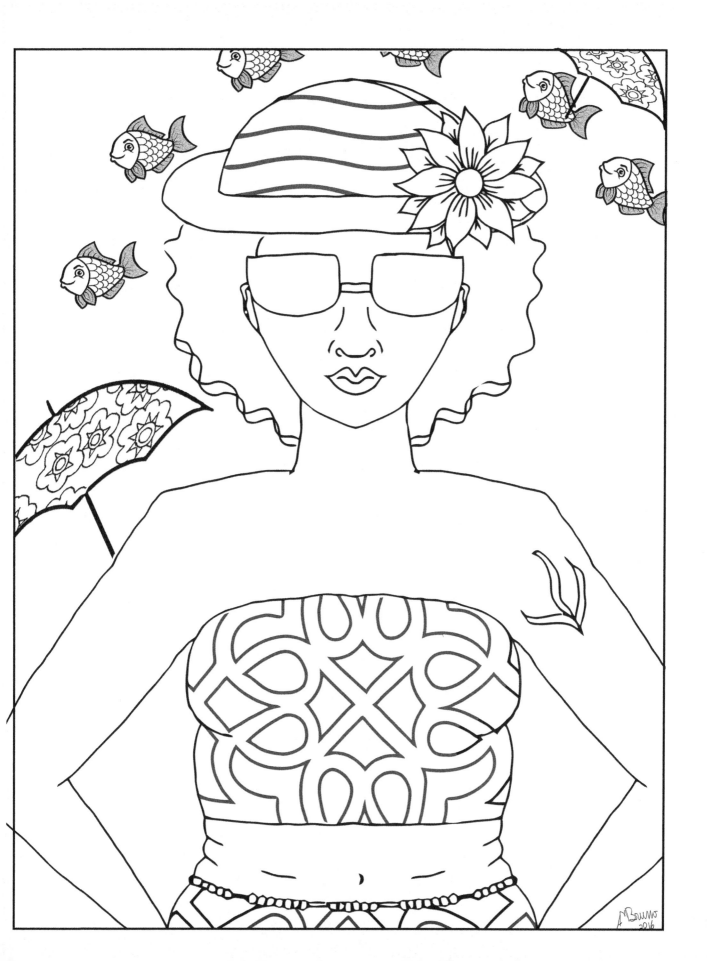

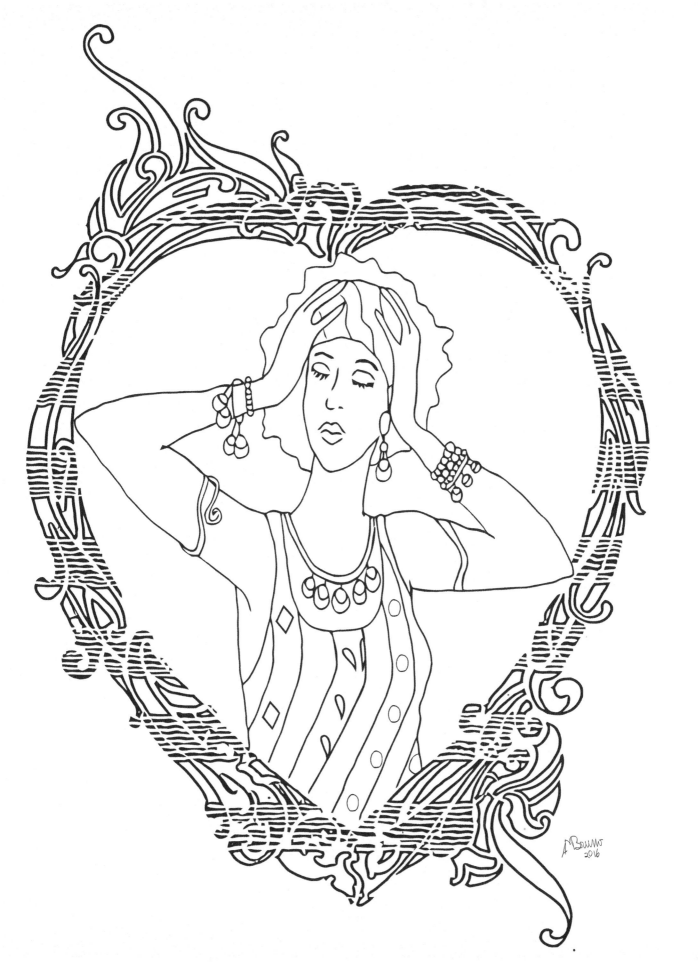

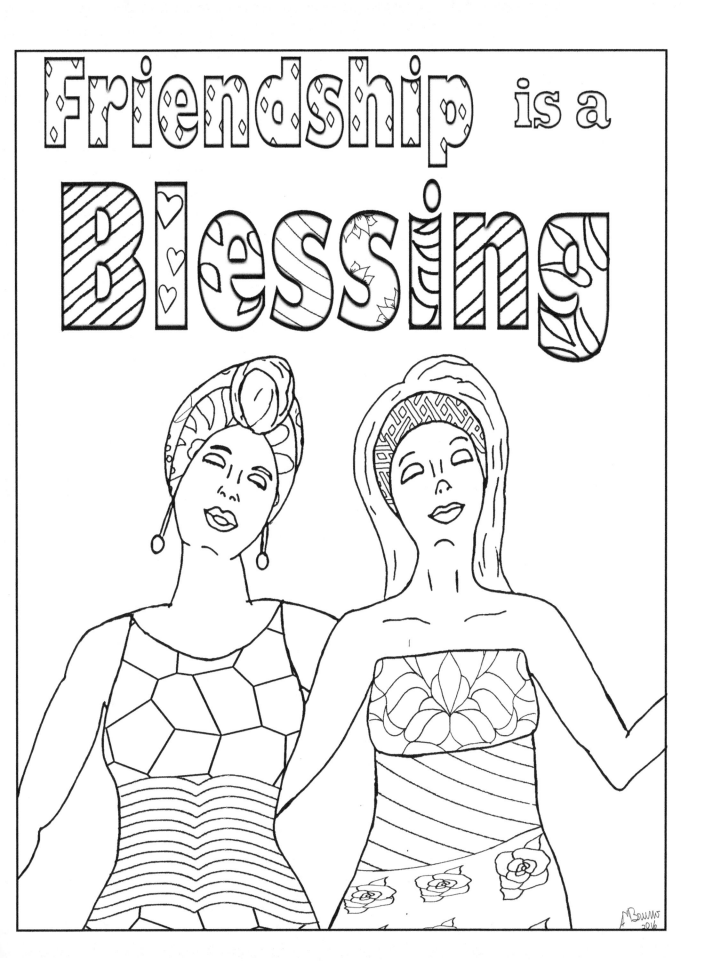

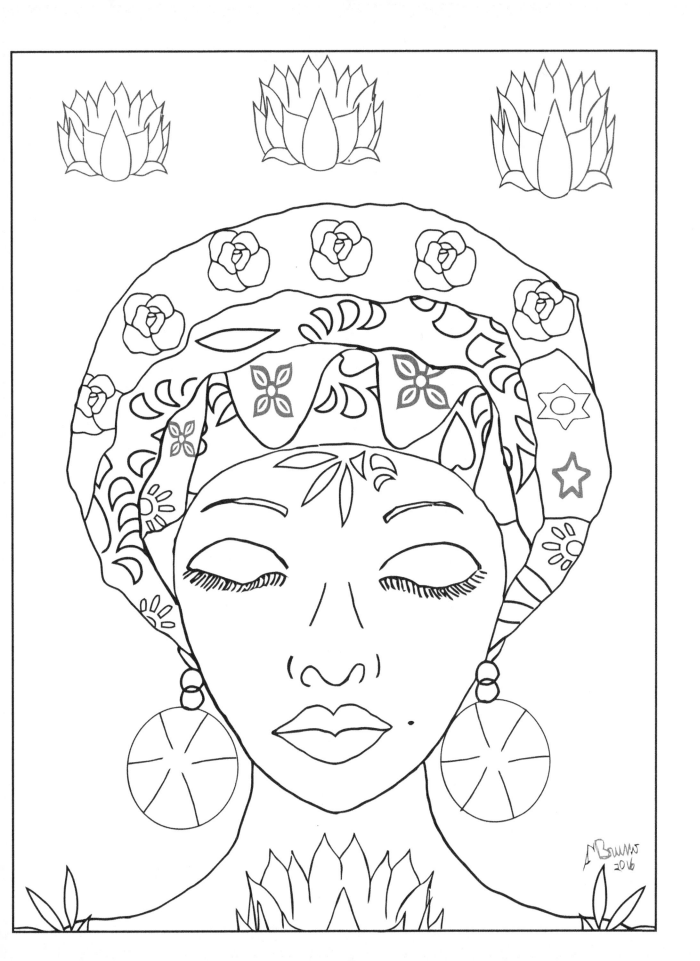

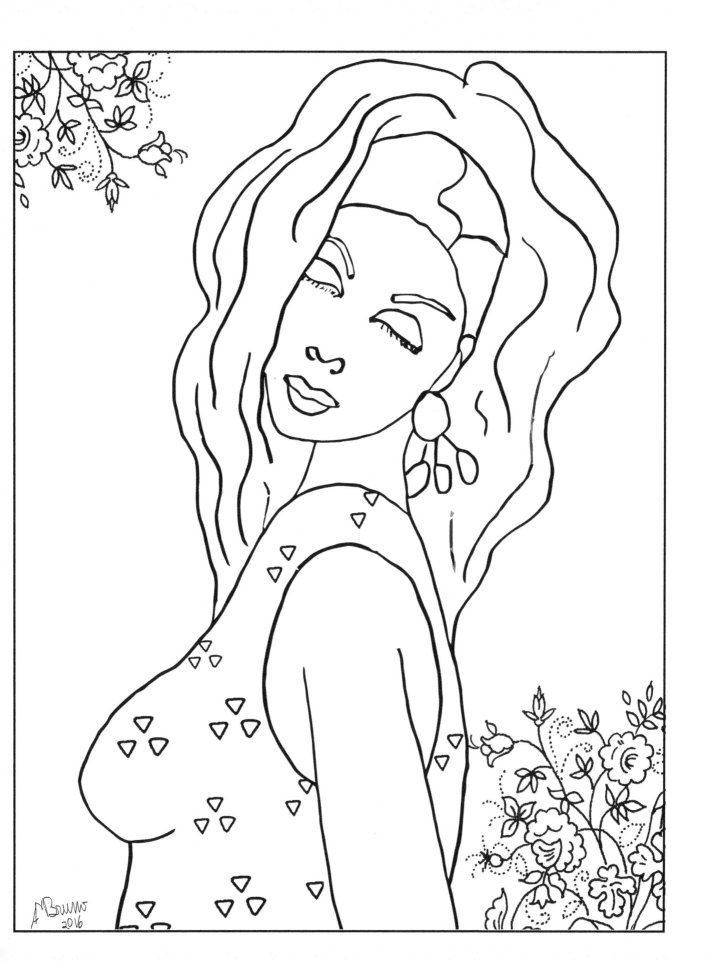

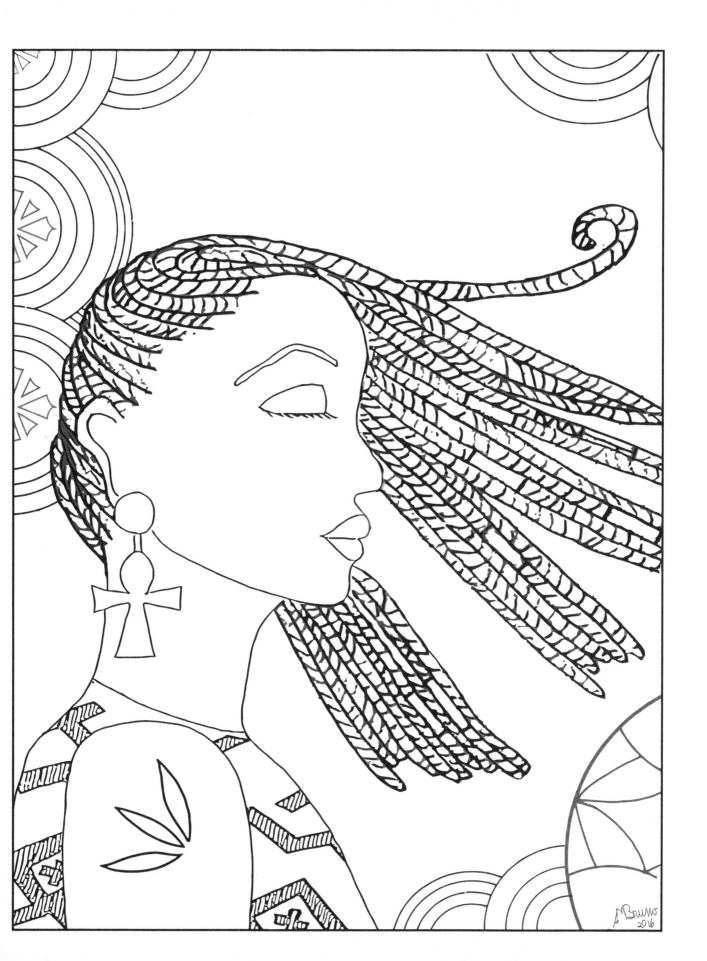

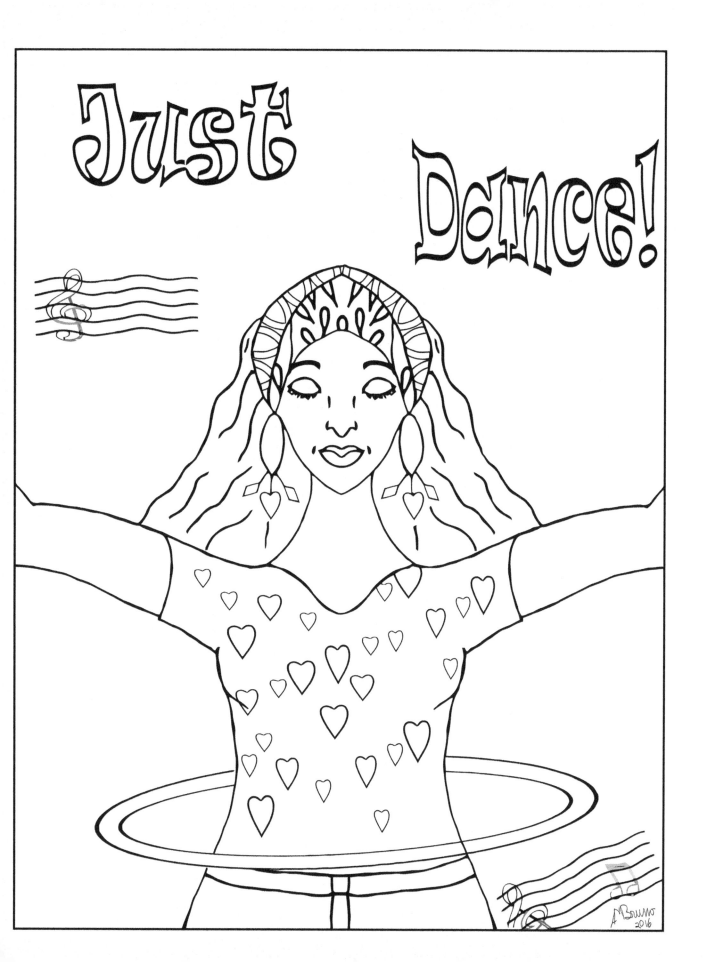

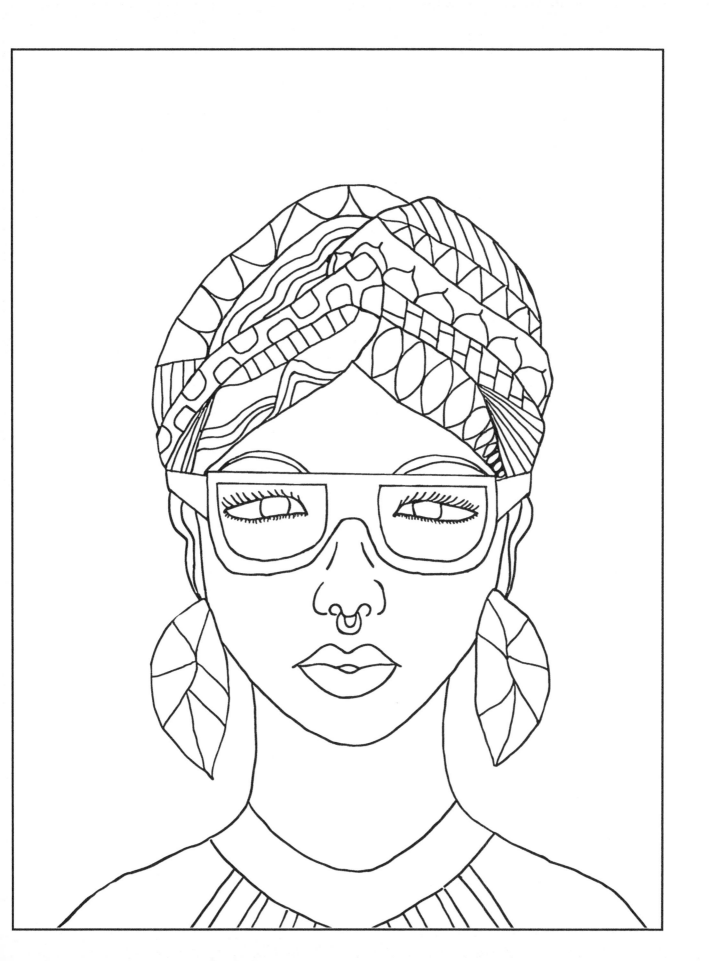

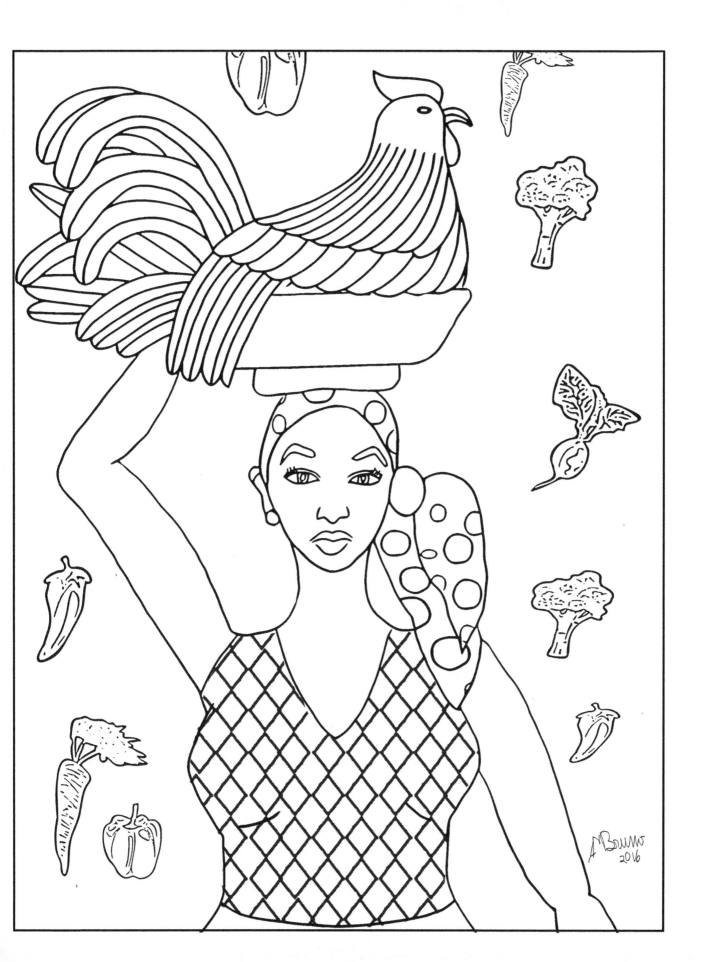

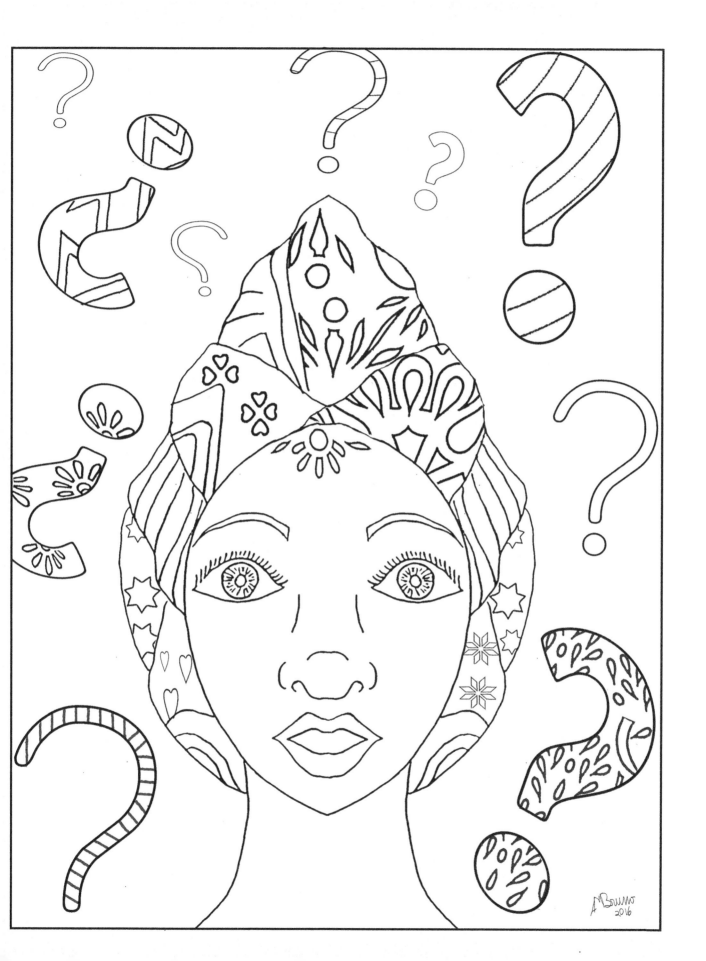

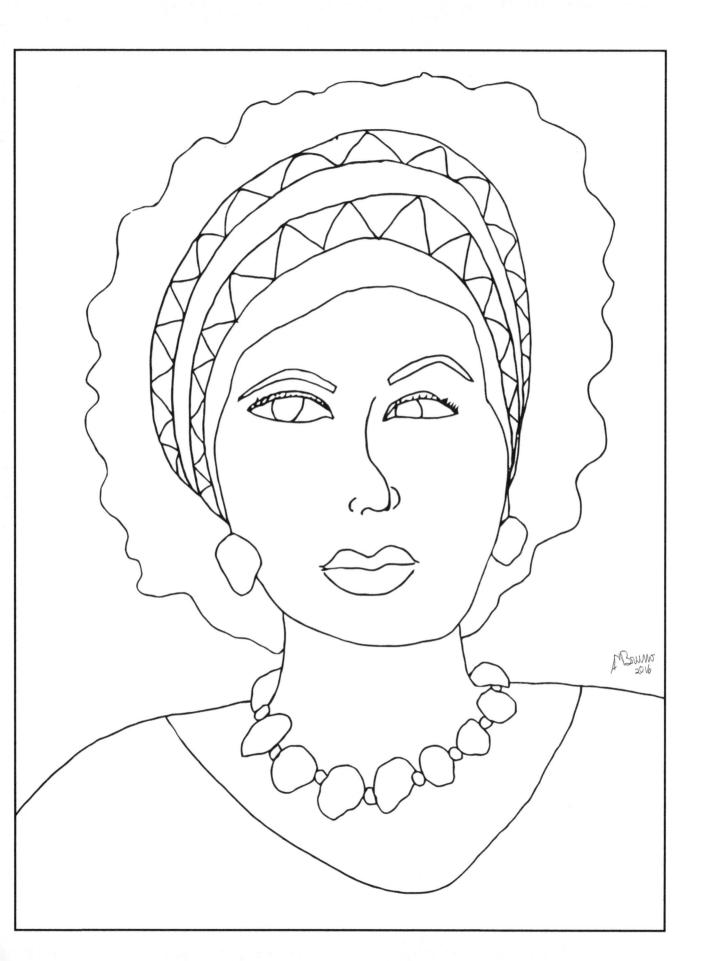

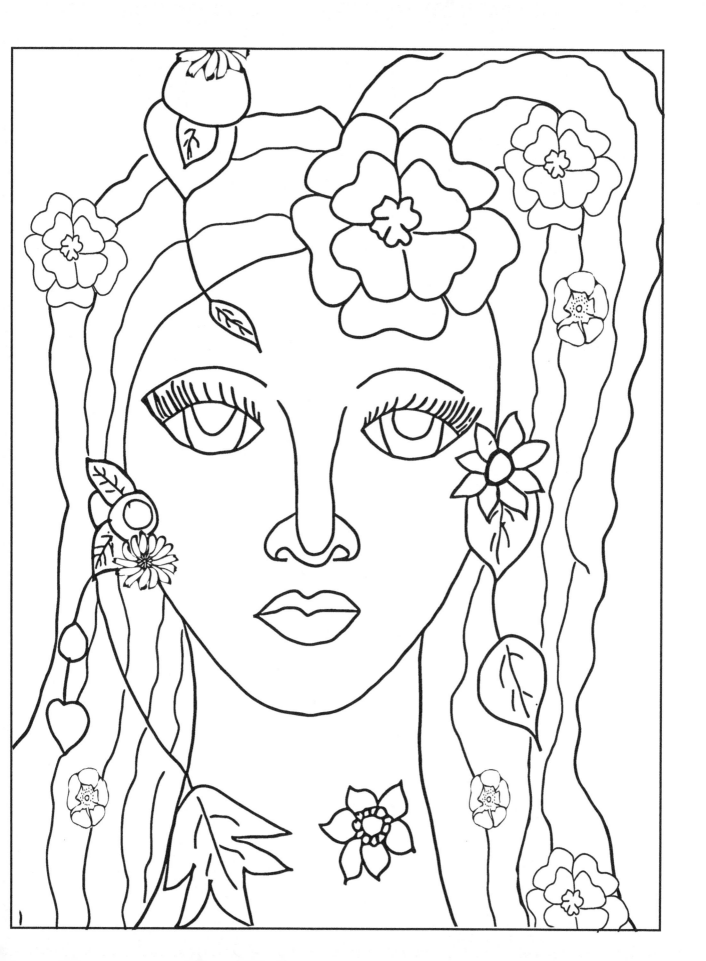

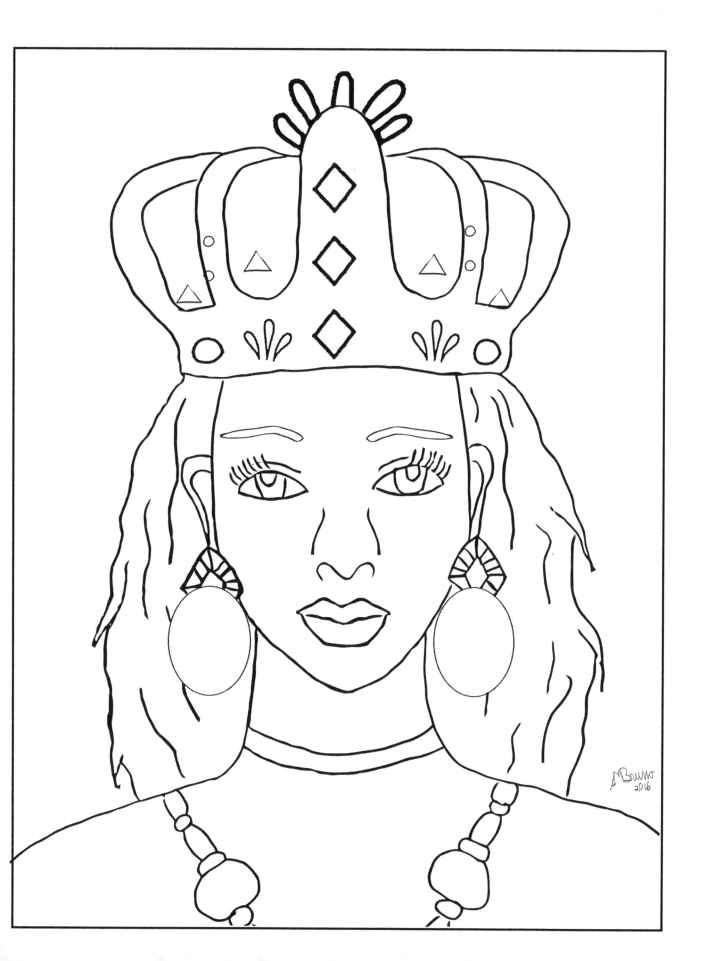

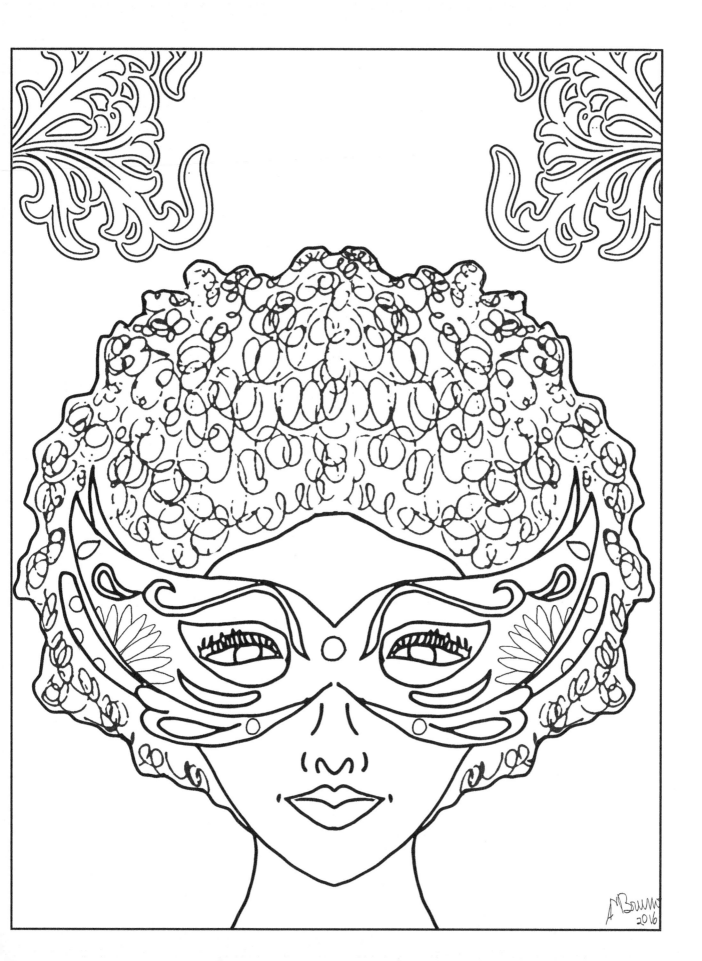

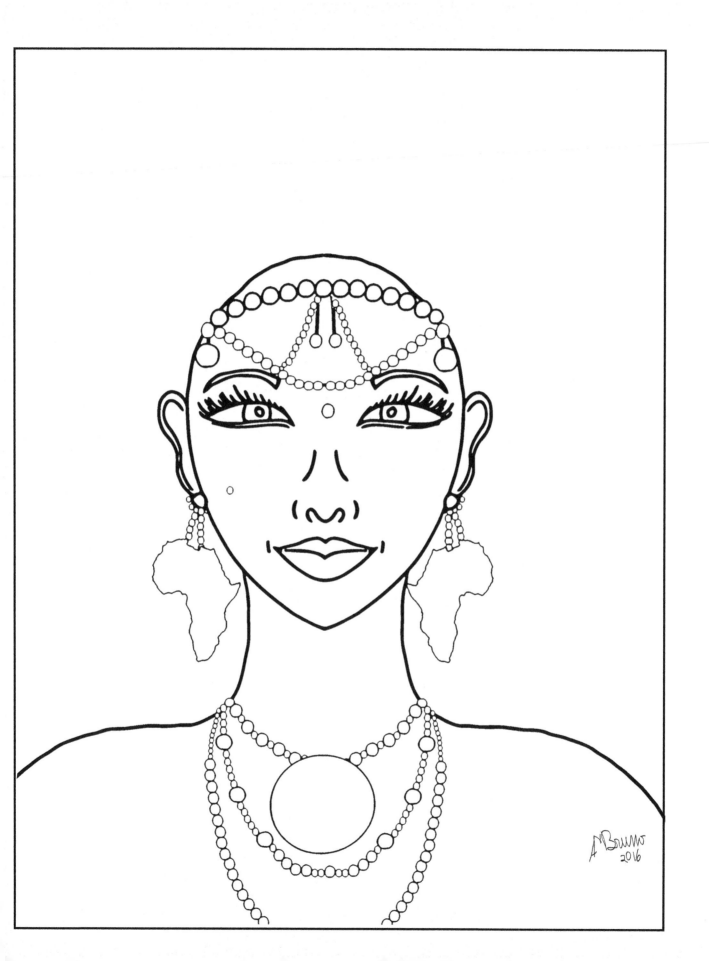

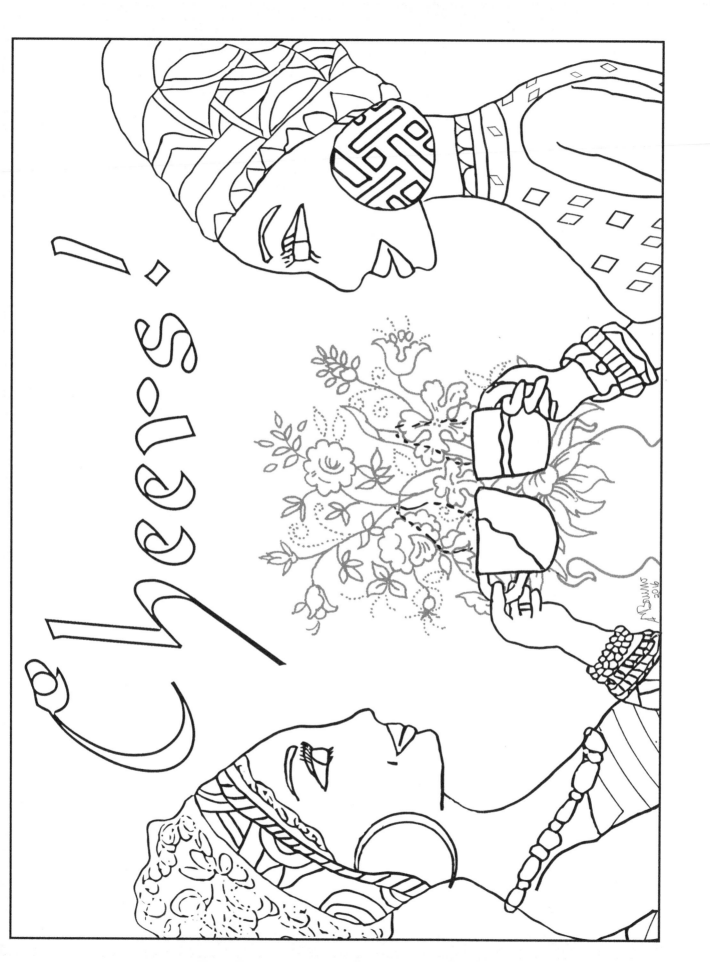

About me

I'm a self-taugth artist who spend most
of my time drawing and painting.
A native of Haiti, my years
spent living in the Dominican Republic
and my travels abroad, as well
as my spiritual and religious views,
have shaped my particular art style.

You can view/purchase more of my
work at :

http:// annebrunoart.com

Made in the USA
Coppell, TX
26 March 2021